SPECTACULAR
SEA CREATURES

by **Niki Catherine**

PENGUIN YOUNG READERS LICENSES
An imprint of Penguin Random House LLC
1745 Broadway, New York, New York 10019

First published in the United States of America by Penguin Young Readers Licenses,
an imprint of Penguin Random House LLC, 2025

TIME for Kids © 2025 TIME USA, LLC. All Rights Reserved.

Visit us online at penguinrandomhouse.com.

Library of Congress Cataloging-in-Publication Data is available.

Manufactured in China

ISBN 9780593888421   10 9 8 7 6 5 4 3 2 1 TOPL

Design by Hsiao-Pin Lin and Abby Dening

. . . .

Photo credits: Cover: Alamy: (anglerfish) Helmut Corneli. **Getty Images:** (clown fish) JodiJacobson/E+, (emperor penguin) AlesVeluscek/E+, (orca) slowmotiongli/iStock, (sea otter) Gerald Corsi/E+, (sea turtle) ShaneMyersPhoto/iStock, (shark) vladoskan/iStock, (tentacle) Studioimagen73/iStock, (water) rami_ba/iStock, (whale tail) empusa/iStock. **Interior: Alamy:** 1: (anglerfish) Helmut Cornel; 8: (top) Doug Perrine; 21: Blue Planet Archive JMI; 26: MARK CONLIN/VWPICS/Visual&Written SL; 30: (bottom) Duncan Murrell; 34: (bottom) Kelvin Aitken/VWPics; 47: (top) Marko Steffensen; 85: Adisha Pramod; 86: Buerkel, D.L./juniors@wildlife/Juniors Bildarchiv GmbH. **Getty Images:** 1: (clown fish) JodiJacobson/E+, (orca) slowmotiongli/iStock, (sea otter) Gerald Corsi/E+, (sea turtle) ShaneMyersPhoto/iStock, (shark) vladoskan/iStock; 5: VitalyEdush/iStock; 6: (top) Andrew Peacock/Stone, (bottom) slowmotiongli/iStock; 7: LaSalle-Photo/iStock; 8: (bottom) pilipenkoD/iStock; 9: (top) Kelly Dalling/iStock, (bottom) C T Aylward/Moment; 11: (top) George Karbus Photography/ Connect Images, (bottom) HUM Images/Universal Images Group; 12: MagicBones/iStock; 13: mirecca/iStock; 14–15: Gerard Soury/The Image Bank; 16: (top) Anne Dirkse/Moment, (bottom) S.Rohrlach/iStock; 17: (top) ifish/iStock, (bottom) Gerard Soury/The Image Bank; 18–19: Patrick Keyser/Moment; 20: (top) Reinhard Dirscherl/The Image Bank, (bottom) Westend61; 22: Dave Collins/iStock; 23: Wirestock/iStock; 24–25: David Merron Photography/Moment; 27: art-design-photography.com/ Moment; 28: Rolf von Riedmatten/imageBROKER; 29: (top) Brent Barnes/Stocktrek Images, (bottom) vojce/iStock; 30: (top) Damocean/iStock; 31: cineuno/iStock; 32: Andrey Nekrasov/imageBROKER; 34: (top) Carla Gottgens/Bloomberg; 35: George D. Lepp/Corbis Documentary; 36: Global_Pics/iStock; 37: Stephen Frink/DigitalVision; 38–39: Alastair Pollock Photography/ Moment; 40: (top) Stephen Frink/The Image Bank, (bottom) Jay Fleming/Corbis Documentary; 41: (top) James Warwick/ The Image Bank, (bottom) Michel VIARD/iStock; 42: Jean Philippe Barbe/500px; 43: (top) Muslianshah Masrie/Photodisc, (bottom) PaulWolf/iStock; 44: Yiming Chen/Moment; 45: Ken Usami/Photodisc; 46: Mlenny/E+; 47: (bottom) Mark Chivers/ imageBROKER; 48: (top) EBMarketa/iStock, (bottom) by wildestanimal/Moment; 49: (top) James R.D. Scott/Moment, (bottom) Sandi Smolker/iStock; 50–51: by wildestanimal/Moment; 52: Dr John A Horsfall/iStock; 53: Damocean/iStock; 54: (top) CoreyFord/iStock, (bottom) Mark Newman/The Image Bank; 55: by wildestanimal/Moment; 56–57: slowmotiongli/ iStock; 58: Kryssia Campos/Moment; 60: mirecca/iStock; 61: Studio-Annika/iStock; 62–63: WhitcombeRD/iStock; 64: (top) johnandersonphoto/iStock, (bottom) katatonia82/iStock; 65: (top) andyKRAKOVSKI/iStock, (bottom) Allexxandar/ iStock; 66–67: by wildestanimal/Moment; 68: stephankerkhofs/iStock; 69: Dan Herrick/Photodisc; 70: LauraDin/iStock; 71: Ed-Ni-Photo/iStock; 72: Ken Kiefer 2/Connect Images; 73: LaSalle-Photo/iStock; 74: Brook Peterson/Stocktrek Images; 75: Wirestock/iStock; 76–77: Verlisia/500px; 78: Damocean/iStock; 79: Tammy616/iStock; 80: Sergio Hanquet/iStock; 81: (top) Gerard Soury/The Image Bank, (bottom) Gerard Soury/Stockbyte; 82: (top) Matt_Potenski/iStock, (bottom) Nigel Marsh/ iStock; 83: Deepshine/iStock; 84: Alastair Pollock Photography/Moment; 87: Jami Tarris/Photodisc; 88–89: 33karen33/E+; 90: torstenvelden/RooM; 91: by wildestanimal/Moment; 92: RibeirodosSantos/iStock; 93: Thomas Kline/Design Pics; 94–95: richcarey/iStock. **Wikimedia Commons:** 10: Dann Blackwood, USGS (public domain); 33: Mike Goren (CC BY 2.0); 59: (top) H. Zell (CC BY-SA 3.0), (bottom) David Csepp, NMFS/AKFSC/ABL (public domain).

CONTENTS

INTRODUCTION

How many sea creatures can you name off the top of your head? Can you count them on your fingers? Despite more than 80 percent of the ocean being unexplored, more than two hundred thousand marine species have already been discovered—and scientists are making new discoveries every day. You would need a *lot* of hands to count all of those critters!

This book will cover 101 sea creatures, from mammals and fish to reptiles and birds. You've probably heard about some of them, but some might be new to you. Maybe you'll find your new favorite sea creature. There are cool deep-sea fish, such as the fangtooth, and gentle giants, like the green sea turtle. There are bus-size giant squid and teeny immortal jellyfish.

While the ocean is massive, it is a very fragile ecosystem. A lot of the big guys rely on tiny creatures as a food source. Those tiny creatures rely on an even tinier food source! Without the littlest guys, the entire ecosystem would collapse.

As you read, think about how each sea creature, no matter its size, has a purpose. Even the smallest creatures have a big role to play.

ADÉLIE PENGUIN
Pygoscelis adeliae

ADÉLIES are medium-size penguins that are incredible walkers, with migrations averaging eight thousand miles. During the winter, they spend most of their time in the sea, using their wings to propel them through the water. Despite being talented swimmers, these penguins don't like to be the first in the water. They'll form tightly packed groups at the water's edge, waiting for someone to fall or be pushed in. Once they see that the first penguin is swimming and the water is safe, the rest will jump in, too.

AFRICAN COELACANTH
Latimeria chalumnae

Before this fish was found by fishermen in deep waters off the coast of southeastern Africa in 1938, it was thought to have been long extinct. The COELACANTH is practically a living fossil. This hard-to-find fish lives up to 2,300 feet below the ocean's surface. Coelacanths can grow up to six and a half feet in length and weigh nearly two hundred pounds.

AMERICAN LOBSTER

Homarus americanus

Also known as the Maine lobster, the **AMERICAN LOBSTER** is the largest crustacean in the world by weight. This sea creature can weigh up to forty-four pounds! Its two front legs are very large claws. One is stronger and used for crushing, and the other is sharper and used for cutting. They help the lobster break up its food. Its diet consists of clams, crabs, fish, and more. The Maine lobster likes to live alone and shelter in rocky areas. Because of their hidden homes, Maine lobsters will eat whatever they happen to find. Their spiny exoskeletons are typically rusty brown in color but have been seen in other colors, like bright blue or green. Like most crustaceans, this lobster must shed its shell in order to grow bigger. But unlike a hermit crab, the Maine lobster doesn't find a new home on the seafloor—it has to grow its own.

ANGLERFISH   **Lophiiformes**

This fish is found in dark, deep-sea environments. It uses a bioluminescent light on its head to hunt its prey. This special light looks quite peculiar. A long, skinny rod stretches out from the head. At the very end of that rod is the bioluminescent light. This light is often referred to as bait because it lures prey toward the **ANGLERFISH**.

ANTARCTIC KRILL

Euphausia superba

This transparent crustacean is one of the most important prey species in the ocean and is the primary food source of many animals. Without it, entire Southern Ocean food chains would collapse. Krill are filter feeders, eating tiny plankton and using their small legs to filter out algae. An **ANTARCTIC KRILL** only weighs about one gram and grows to be just a little over two inches long. These bioluminescent creatures are nocturnal, so they come to the surface at night to feed. They then move to the ocean depths to rest during the day. There are more than seven hundred trillion of these crustaceans in the Southern Ocean.

ATLANTIC BLUE MARLIN

Makaira nigricans

The **ATLANTIC BLUE MARLIN** is one of the fastest fish in the sea, moving at up to sixty-eight miles per hour. It can grow up to fourteen feet in length and weigh more than 1,900 pounds. With its long spear-shaped upper jaw (called a bill), it swims through schools of fish at high speeds and slashes its jaw around to stun its prey. Then it goes back to eat.

ATLANTIC PUFFIN

Fratercula arctica

The **ATLANTIC PUFFIN** lives at sea for most of its life. It uses its webbed feet to steer like boat rudders and its wings like paddles to propel itself forward. This small seabird can soar, too, flapping its wings up to four hundred times a minute. It can fly at speeds of forty-eight to fifty-five miles per hour. That's as fast as a car on a highway. It can dive up to two hundred feet underwater looking for food.

ATLANTIC SEA SCALLOP

Placopecten magellanicus

This mollusk consists of two smooth, saucer-shaped shells with scalloped edges. Its coloring is typically reddish pink or brown on top, and white on the bottom. Unlike clams and oysters, scallops can propel themselves through the water by snapping their shells open and shut. This helps them escape predators. They feed on phytoplankton. By eating phytoplankton, **ATLANTIC SEA SCALLOPS** actually filter the water they live in and make it cleaner. They can be thanked for improving water quality with their eating habits.

BASKING SHARK
Cetorhinus maximus

Although the **BASKING SHARK** is the second-largest fish in the world, it is calm and harmless. As a filter feeder, it spends most of its time near the surface with its mouth hanging open, filtering food out of the water. It can filter around two thousand tons of water every hour. Though it has about 1,500 teeth, the basking shark doesn't use them for feeding. Some scientists believe that these tiny teeth are instead used as part of the mating process. Basking sharks weigh up to about ten thousand pounds and can reach an average of twenty-six feet in length.

BLOBFISH
Psychrolutes marcidus

Not much is known about this frowning, flabby bottom-feeder because it lives extremely deep in the ocean. It has soft bones and a jellylike body that allows it to float just above the seafloor, waiting for prey to pass by. Then the **BLOBFISH** gobbles it up with its large mouth. Though it looks like a deflated balloon when it is brought to the surface, the blobfish looks more like other fish when it's down in its natural habitat.

BLUE MUSSELS

Mytilus edulis

Found on rocky shores, **BLUE MUSSELS** use their strong threadlike appendages to attach to rocky surfaces, crevices, and piers in dense groups. These groups form a colony, or bed, that includes creatures like worms, crustaceans, and other invertebrates. Like clams and oysters, mussels are harvested for food. These sea creatures are usually between two and four inches long. In a single spawning event, a female blue mussel might produce up to two hundred million eggs.

BLUESPOTTED RIBBONTAIL RAY

Taeniura lymma

The **BLUESPOTTED RIBBONTAIL RAY** is small for a ray, growing only twelve to fourteen inches long, with yellow-brown coloring and bright blue spots. It has two venomous spines on its tail but typically uses them only for self-defense. Like many of us, this ray would rather run away from a fight! It keeps close to the seafloor where it feeds, digging in the sand with its mouth, hunting for shrimp and crabs. It uses sensing organs that pick up on the electrical fields and temperature changes around it to help it locate prey.

FUN FACT: At birth, a baby blue whale is already twenty-three feet long and weighs up to six thousand pounds. Because of this, the mother whale must produce more than fifty gallons of milk a day to feed her massive baby.

BLUE WHALE

Balaenoptera musculus

Growing up to one hundred feet long and weighing up to two hundred tons (which is four hundred thousand pounds), the **BLUE WHALE** is the largest animal on earth! Its heart can weigh as much as a car, and its tongue weighs as much as an elephant. Despite its incredible size, a blue whale's diet is mainly krill. It eats up to four tons of krill a day. Its coloring looks light blue underwater, which is where the name *blue whale* comes from. The blue whale is very vocal, producing sounds that can be louder than a jet engine. Due to hunting, blue whales are endangered. There are only between ten thousand and twenty-five thousand left in the wild. Many different groups, like Ocean Alliance, work to conserve the remaining blue whales by reducing the risk of fishing net accidents, promoting whale-safe shipping practices, and working to reduce ocean noise.

BLUE-FOOTED BOOBY

Sula nebouxii

Found off the western coasts of Central and South America, these marine birds are known and named for their bright blue feet. Males like to show off their feet to potential mates with a fancy little walk. The name *booby* comes from the Spanish word *bobo*, which means "foolish" or "clown." The **BLUE-FOOTED BOOBY** earned this bobo-based name because it is, like other seabirds, clumsy on land. However, these birds are skilled fliers and can make dives into the water from as high as eighty feet in the air when they're looking for food.

BLUE GLAUCUS SEA SLUG

Glaucus atlanticus

By feeding on venomous prey, the **BLUE GLAUCUS SEA SLUG** becomes toxic itself. It floats upside down on the water. Its blue underbelly helps it blend into the water's surface, while its gray back helps it blend into the water when seen from below. This coloring is called countershading. It helps the creature hide from both flying and swimming predators.

BOGUE FISH

Boops boops

This sea creature is named for its big, buggy eyes. The **BOGUE FISH** can reach about fourteen inches in length. These fish like to feed in schools at the water's surface at night, munching on seaweed, crustaceans, and plankton. Schools of bogue fish are usually found about five hundred feet below the surface. The scientific name sounds a bit silly: *Boops boops!* This name actually comes from the Greek word for *cow eye*.

BULL SHARK

Carcharhinus leucas

While sharks need salt water to survive, **BULL SHARKS** have the special ability to live in fresh water, too. They're the most dangerous and aggressive sharks in the world, spending time around highly populated shorelines and busy beaches. They are one of the sharks most likely to attack humans. Mostly, they eat small sharks, bony fish, turtles, birds, dolphins, and sometimes even other bull sharks.

CALIFORNIA SEA LION

Zalophus californianus

The **SEA LION** is a type of sea creature called a pinniped. Pinnipeds are marine animals that have front and rear flippers. Seals, walruses, and sea lions are all pinnipeds. A sea lion's rear flippers help it swim. It has blubber to keep itself warm. The small flaps on each side of a sea lion's head keep water out of its ears. When sea lions are scooting around on land, they hang out in large groups on rocks and sandy shores. These sea creatures go into the water to cool off and feed. While they have teeth, they really only use them for defense against other creatures. Sea lions prefer to swallow their food whole in one huge bite! They don't need to drink water, as they get all the water they need from their food.

FUN FACT: A group of sea lions in the water is called a raft.

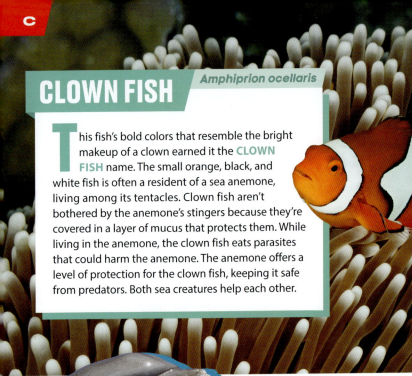

CLOWN FISH

Amphiprion ocellaris

This fish's bold colors that resemble the bright makeup of a clown earned it the **CLOWN FISH** name. The small orange, black, and white fish is often a resident of a sea anemone, living among its tentacles. Clown fish aren't bothered by the anemone's stingers because they're covered in a layer of mucus that protects them. While living in the anemone, the clown fish eats parasites that could harm the anemone. The anemone offers a level of protection for the clown fish, keeping it safe from predators. Both sea creatures help each other.

COMMON BOTTLENOSE DOLPHIN

Tursiops truncatus

When **COMMON BOTTLENOSE DOLPHINS** are born, they create their own special whistle that they use like a name. They are very playful, spending their time surfing waves and following boats. They can produce squeaks and clicks to communicate, but they also use body language. They are very active creatures and can leap twenty feet in the air.

COOKIECUTTER SHARK

Isistius brasiliensis

This small shark is named for the way it feeds, like a parasite, chomping off small chunks of much larger animals, including spinner dolphins and great white sharks. It uses its sharp, pointed upper teeth and suction-cup lips to latch on and its thick triangular lower teeth to scoop out a piece, leaving a round chunk missing from the larger creature. The **COOKIECUTTER SHARK** got its name because this process looks similar to when a cookie cutter takes a small shape out of a larger sheet of dough. These sharks have a small tube-shaped body, and their underbelly is covered in tiny bioluminescent organs, so their bodies glow.

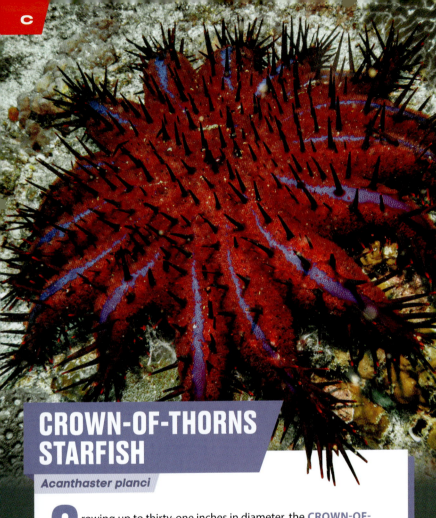

CROWN-OF-THORNS STARFISH

Acanthaster planci

Growing up to thirty-one inches in diameter, the **CROWN-OF-THORNS STARFISH** is quite large for a starfish. It also has a deadly reputation. It can have up to twenty-one arms, all covered in venomous spines. At feeding time, it can push its stomach out of its mouth and consume a soft tissue layer from the coral. When it is done, it pulls its stomach back into its body. Due to huge population outbreaks, crown-of-thorns starfish are responsible for massive coral loss on the Great Barrier Reef. Humans have often removed crown-of-thorns starfish from reefs to save the coral.

DUMBO OCTOPUS

Grimpoteuthis spp.

The **DUMBO OCTOPUS** is named for the fins on top of its head that resemble Dumbo the elephant, who is famous for his big ears. It flaps those very fins to help propel itself through water. It lives in the deep open ocean at depths of up to thirteen thousand feet, making it the deepest dweller of all known octopuses. This small octopus reaches only about twelve inches in size, which is the length of a ruler. Even though it is small, it still has about sixty-five suction cups along each arm.

EMPEROR PENGUIN

Aptenodytes forsteri

This flightless bird is found only in Antarctica in large colonies. It is considered to be the Olympic diver of the bird world, diving up to 1,800 feet and staying underwater for up to twenty minutes at a time. After a female **EMPEROR PENGUIN** lays its egg, the male protects the egg by balancing it on his feet and covering it with his brood pouch, which is a special flap of skin, to keep it warm. He stands like that for about sixty-five days. When the female penguin returns home with food to regurgitate for her now hatched baby, the male then goes on his own fishing journey. These penguins are kept warm by two layers of feathers on their bodies, and they have special fat in their feet to keep them from freezing.

FUN FACT: Colonies of emperor penguins can be seen all the way from space. That's a lot of penguins!

FANGTOOTH

Anoplogaster cornuta

This sharp-toothed fish is one of the deepest-dwelling of the deep-sea fishes. It can be found at depths of sixteen thousand feet, though it is known to move to shallower water at night to feed. Rather than wait around to ambush its prey, the **FANGTOOTH** goes looking for food and uses its huge mouth to suck its prey inside whole. Then, it kills the prey with its huge teeth. It has special pouches in its mouth that protect its brain from being stabbed by its own pointy teeth.

FLAMBOYANT CUTTLEFISH

Metasepia pfefferi

Instead of swimming, the small **FLAMBOYANT CUTTLEFISH** actually walks along the seafloor. It has eight arms and two tentacles. Flamboyant cuttlefish only grow to be about three inches in length. Though they are mostly brown in color, they have touches of yellow and purple on their arms. These cuttlefish also have special cells in their skin that allow them to change color. When threatened, these sea creatures release clouds of ink to escape predators and use their color-changing ability to camouflage.

FLAMINGO TONGUE SNAIL

Cyphoma gibbosum

The bright pink or orange coloring and black rings of this snail warn predators to keep away. That is because this little snail is toxic. That means sea creatures can be poisoned and die if they consume **FLAMINGO TONGUE SNAILS**. These snails slowly crawl along soft corals, eating away at them. The toxins from the coral they eat are what make the snails toxic. They then get to use those toxins for self-defense.

FLYING FISH

Exocoetidae

Found in warm ocean waters all over the world, this torpedo-shaped fish uses its winglike pectoral fins to glide through the air. **FLYING FISH** swim up to thirty-seven miles per hour in order to break through the surface of the water and propel themselves into the air. They can fly distances of up to 655 feet and reach heights of over four feet, often becoming targets for airborne predators such as seabirds.

FUN FACT: Some small fish and even small crabs will ride around on the fried egg jellyfish.

FRIED EGG JELLYFISH

Cotylorhiza tuberculata

Is it breakfast time? Most commonly found in the Mediterranean Sea, the **FRIED EGG JELLYFISH** is named for its resemblance to an egg yolk. It spends most of its time motionless, slowly pulsing its flattened, disc-shaped body (also known as a bell) while drifting in the open sea. Deep purple tentacles are used to capture prey, eat, and defend the jellyfish against predators.

GIANT CARIBBEAN SEA ANEMONE

Condylactis gigantea

This large anemone is found in coral reefs all throughout the Caribbean. Though they look stationary, these **GIANT CARIBBEAN SEA ANEMONES** actually crawl around very slowly, feeding on fish and crustaceans that get too close to their tentacles. When they're threatened, they pull into a tight ball, which makes it difficult for predators to attack them. They come in a variety of colors, such as light blue, white, pink, orange, and red. Anemones have friendly relationships with some fish, giving them a place to live and protection.

GIANT DEVIL RAY

Mobula mobular

These rays are known for leaping from the ocean using their long, winglike fins. As filter feeders, **GIANT DEVIL RAYS** catch their food while they swim. This means that they take in a *lot* of water all day, filtering out the tiny plankton and other nutrients from the water in order to eat. They have a black crescent-shaped stripe that stretches from shoulder to shoulder, and they are typically six to nine feet wide.

GIANT OCEANIC MANTA RAY

Mobula birostris

The **GIANT OCEANIC MANTA RAY** is not only the largest ray—it's one of the largest fish in the world, reaching a wingspan of up to twenty-nine feet. It is constantly swimming and does so with its large mouth hanging open so it can filter in plankton and other small food as it moves. Its specialized winglike fins help direct more water and food into the manta's mouth as its goes. It has one of the largest brains of any fish. It can even recognize itself in a mirror! Its large, flat, diamond-shaped body is typically black or black with a white belly.

GIANT PACIFIC OCTOPUS

Enteroctopus dofleini

The largest of all octopuses, this reddish-pink mollusk (a type of animal with a soft, unsegmented body, and often a shell) can grow to be around sixteen feet from tip to tip and weigh more than fifty pounds. Despite being color-blind, these creatures have special pigment cells called chromatophores that let them change color to blend in with their surroundings. This is how they camouflage! Along with their three hearts, they have eight arms covered in more than two thousand suction cups that give them a superstrong grip. With their nine brains, **GIANT PACIFIC OCTOPUSES** are known to be very smart animals.

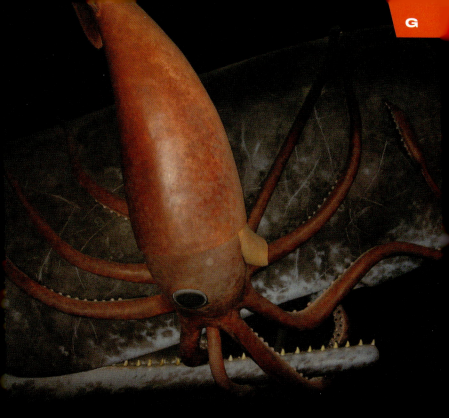

GIANT SQUID

Architeuthis dux

Rarely seen by humans, the **GIANT SQUID** can grow to be almost as long as a school bus, at an average of thirty-three feet long. This makes them the biggest invertebrate on earth. An invertebrate is an animal without a backbone. The giant squid's eyes are the size of basketballs and help them see in the deep, dark depths they live in, where there is little to no light. In addition to their eight arms, they have two longer whiplike tentacles that help them capture prey, including shrimp and other squid. Giant squid are so large and spectacular that some people believe that those who thought they had seen a mythical creature called the kraken centuries ago had actually seen a giant squid.

GIANT TIGER PRAWN

Penaeus monodon

The **GIANT TIGER PRAWN** is named for the striped pattern on its body that is unique like tiger stripes. It lives on soft ocean floors, eating up algae, plants, and invertebrates. It is nocturnal, burying itself in sand during the day and emerging to feed at night. Adults can reach up to thirteen inches long but females are typically larger than the males.

GOBLIN SHARK

Mitsukurina owstoni

The **GOBLIN SHARK** has a long, narrow snout and an unusual jaw that unhinges during feedings. All of its fang-like teeth do not fit in its odd mouth, so they are visible even when the mouth is closed. Its snout is covered in special organs that help it locate prey in the dark, which is important since goblin sharks live deep in the ocean.

GRAY WHALE

Eschrichtius robustus

The **GRAY WHALE** is known for making lengthy migrations. It can travel more than twelve thousand miles on its journey from its summer habitat to its winter habitat and then back to its summer habitat. A habitat is where an animal lives, and some animals have different habitats for different seasons to avoid freezing temperatures. The gray whale's snout and back are often covered in over four hundred pounds of barnacles and other tiny creatures. Using its snout to forage, it kicks up the seafloor and filters water through its comblike plates, called baleen, in its mouth. The baleen helps to strain out the food from the water so that the whale can eat it. Gray whales can grow to be forty-nine feet long and weigh up to eighty thousand pounds.

GREAT BARRACUDA

Sphyraena barracuda

With a body that cuts through the water like a torpedo, the **GREAT BARRACUDA** can swim up to thirty-six miles per hour and is one of the fastest animals in the ocean. It spends most of its time swimming slowly in order to conserve energy for when it wants to sneak up on its prey. Because of its speed and size, it has very few predators, and tends to live on its own. It is an aggressive animal, and it sometimes steals fish from human divers.

GREAT HAMMERHEAD SHARK

Sphyrna mokarran

The **GREAT HAMMERHEAD SHARK** is the largest of all nine hammerhead species, growing to lengths of up to twenty feet. Because of the wide shape of its head with eyes at each end, it's able to see with a wider perspective than other sea creatures. Its head also contains sensory organs that allow the shark to detect prey in its surroundings. Once it spots a victim, it uses its head to pin its food down to the ocean floor. It mainly eats stingrays and doesn't often hunt sea creatures bigger than those.

GREAT WHITE SHARK

Carcharodon carcharias

GREAT WHITE SHARKS are recognizable for their torpedo-shaped bodies and white underbellies. They can grow up to twenty-one feet long and weigh over four thousand pounds. These sharks are the largest predatory fish on earth, which puts them at the very top of the food chain. They have a set of three hundred sharp triangular teeth in seven rows that they use to catch their prey, which includes sea lions, seals, and even small whales. A great white shark can smell a single drop of blood in twenty-five gallons of water. Great white sharks are often featured as villains in movies, such as *Jaws*. While they're famous for attacking humans in these films, there are actually only five to ten reported fatal great white shark attacks a year. In most cases, these sharks prefer to keep to themselves.

FUN FACT: In the Pixar movie *Finding Nemo*, Bruce is a great white shark.

GREEN MORAY EEL

Gymnothorax funebris

Found in the Atlantic Ocean, the **GREEN MORAY EEL** is one of the largest of the moray eel species. Its green color comes from a unique layer of mucus that protects it from parasites and diseases. Green moray eels are long and flat. They have one long dorsal fin that runs the length of their body. They're nocturnal, spending their days hiding in crevices and waiting to hunt for food at night. This eel can wrap itself around its prey, tying itself into a knot!

GREEN SEA TURTLE

Chelonia mydas

The **GREEN SEA TURTLE** gets its name from the greenish color of its fat, which comes from its plant-based diet of seagrass and algae. It travels long distances in its lifetime and uses the earth's magnetic field like an invisible map to navigate its many journeys. The second-largest of all sea turtles, these creatures can grow to be up to five feet long and up to seven hundred pounds. While they spend most of their time underwater, green sea turtles in Hawaii like to come ashore to sunbathe.

H

HARBOR SEAL
Phoca vitulina

When **HARBOR SEALS** are on land, they bounce around from place to place in a caterpillar-like crawl. In the sea, they are graceful swimmers. They typically stay close to home, splitting their time between land and sea, and spend up to 85 percent of their day foraging for food. They are found in both fresh- and saltwater environments and enjoy basking in the sun.

HARP SEAL
Pagophilus groenlandicus

The **HARP SEAL** is named for the curved black patch on its back that resembles the shape of a harp. When the harp seal is born, it is covered in white fur, which helps it absorb sunlight to stay warm in the Arctic. But as it grows, it sheds its white fur and replaces it with gray fur. Harp seals spend most of their time diving and swimming. They can dive 1,300 feet, staying underwater for up to sixteen minutes at a time.

41

HERMIT CRAB

Pagurus spp.

These small crabs like to use empty snail shells and other hollow objects as shelter and protection for their soft bodies. Without that protection, they are very vulnerable to predators. As the crab grows, it must find and move into a new, larger shell, and sometimes even fight other crabs for a specific shell if there are limited options. HERMIT CRABS are more closely related to some kinds of lobsters than to true crabs, which grow their own shells.

HORSESHOE CRAB
Limulidae

HORSESHOE CRABS are actually more closely related to scorpions and spiders than to crabs. They've been around for more than four hundred million years, making them older than dinosaurs. Horseshoe crabs earned their name thanks to their round, horseshoe-shaped heads. They have a hard exoskeleton, nine eyes, and ten legs that they use to walk on the seafloor. This sea creature has a long, pointed tail, called a telson, that looks menacing but is mostly used to flip the crab over if it happens to end up on its back.

HUMPBACK WHALE
Megaptera novaeangliae

These powerful swimmers are filter feeders who eat krill and other tiny fish. HUMPBACK WHALES are named for their recognizable humps. These whales can grow up to sixty-two feet long and weigh up to eighty thousand pounds. Due to their size, one of their only predators is the orca. They are most well-known for their whale songs.

IMMORTAL JELLYFISH

Turritopsis dohrnii

This jellyfish is only about four and a half millimeters across fully grown, making it smaller than a pinkie fingernail. Despite being so tiny, the jelly's transparent bell has ninety tentacles. When faced with danger or injury, the **IMMORTAL JELLYFISH** has the ability to age backward—a process called transdifferentiation—turning the fully grown jelly back into a polyp and starting the aging process over again from the beginning. Can you imagine if you could turn back into a baby like an immortal jellyfish?

JAPANESE SPIDER CRAB

Macrocheira kaempferi

This crab is a scavenger on the seafloor. It travels easily over mud with its long, limber legs, searching for dead fish to eat. It has ten legs: eight for walking and two with claws for grabbing. If a **JAPANESE SPIDER CRAB** happens to lose a leg to a predator, the leg can regrow when the crab sheds its shell for a new one. This shell shedding is part of a process called molting. The Japanese spider crab is the largest crab on earth, with a leg span reaching up to twelve feet from claw to claw. This crab is named for its spindly resemblance to a spider.

KING PENGUIN

Aptenodytes patagonicus

The **KING PENGUIN** is the largest penguin outside Antarctica and the second-largest penguin on earth, weighing up to forty-five pounds. It has bright orange patches of feathers on its head. The king penguin prefers rocky shores near the ocean to snow and ice. Males and females take turns protecting their egg, keeping it warm in their brood pouch while the other goes fishing for food.

LANTERNFISH
Myctophidae

Found in oceans worldwide, this small fish has a little bioluminescent organ on its nose that acts similarly to a car's headlight, helping the fish see where it is going and what is in its path. Every night the **LANTERNFISH** takes a journey to the surface to look for its favorite food: zooplankton. It does this in such large numbers that the group often appears as one solid mass on sonar.

LEAF SHEEP
Costasiella kuroshimae

This slug can photosynthesize, turning light into nutrients, like a plant does. This isn't the only way **LEAF SHEEP** slugs are similar to plants . . . they look like plants, too! Covered in leaflike appendages, this slug is only about one centimeter in length and gets its green coloring from munching on green algae. It is slow moving and spends most of its life on a type of green algae that it can blend in with, so it stays out of danger by remaining unseen.

LEAFY SEA DRAGON

Phycodurus eques

This large sea dragon is not the best swimmer, so it relies on its camouflaging abilities to escape predators. This is easier thanks to its leaflike appendages, which can easily blend in with seaweed and seagrass since they are green and brown. The **LEAFY SEA DRAGON** likes to flow with the current, blending in even better with the vegetation surrounding it.

LEATHERBACK SEA TURTLE

Dermochelys coriacea

Named for its tough, rubbery, leatherlike shell, the **LEATHERBACK SEA TURTLE** is the largest turtle in the world. It can weigh up to two thousand pounds. That's as heavy as a large bison! It prefers deep ocean waters and can hold its breath for more than an hour when it dives to depths up to 4,200 feet. Between its nest and its foraging adventures, this turtle can swim more than ten thousand miles a year. These amazing ocean dwellers have been around since dinosaurs roamed the earth.

LION'S MANE JELLYFISH

Cyanea capillata

Talk about a "mane" event! The **LION'S MANE JELLYFISH** is named for the long, hairlike tentacles that hang from the underside of its bell. Each jellyfish can have up to 1,200 of them, and they can reach 120 feet long. The tentacles contain poison that makes for a toxic sting that is used to attack prey and defend against predators. The jelly has bioluminescent ability, which means it's able to produce its own light and glow in the dark.

LOGGERHEAD SEA TURTLE

Caretta caretta

The **LOGGERHEAD SEA TURTLE** uses its large log-like head and powerful jaws to crush the hard shells of its prey, which include queen conches and crustaceans. It also likes to eat softer creatures, such as jellyfish and seaweed. Loggerheads have a reddish-brown, heart-shaped shell and a pale-yellow underbelly. They can swim up to fifteen miles per hour, which is three times as fast as an Olympic swimmer!

MARINE IGUANA

Amblyrhynchus cristatus

Found only in the Galápagos Islands, **MARINE IGUANAS** are the only lizards on earth that spend time in the ocean. They swim with a snakelike slither in shallow ocean waters, feeding on marine algae along the shore and seafloor. When they're not feeding, they spend most of their time on land, basking in the warm sun to raise their body temperature and collect enough energy to swim. Once they are in the water, their heartbeat slows to half its normal pace so they can conserve energy.

FUN FACT: These iguanas sneeze out salt that their bodies have filtered out of their blood. Getting rid of excess salt helps prevent dehydration.

MARINE OTTER
Lontra felina

Also known as sea cats, **MARINE OTTERS** spend most of their time in the water. They're not only the smallest otters but the smallest marine mammal. On average, they weigh between six and eleven pounds. These otters have short tails and webbed feet, with stiff whiskers above their upper lips. Their fur is thick and provides insulation. While they are great swimmers, they are also amazing rock climbers. They live in the waters of the South American coast on the southwestern side of the continent.

MOON JELLY *Aurelia aurita*

Commonly hunted by leatherback sea turtles, **MOON JELLYFISH** are usually found near the coast, where there are higher levels of human activity. More humans means fewer predators and more prey! Moon jellyfish are not strong swimmers, so they often wash up on beaches. Named for its see-through, moonlike bell, a moon jelly has short tentacles that sting, and the bell can appear in a range of colors, including pinks and blues.

NARWHAL
Monodon monoceros

Nicknamed the unicorn of the sea, **NARWHALS** have a spiral, ivory toothlike tusk that reaches out ten feet from their mouths. The tooth is covered in nerves and tiny holes that allow seawater to enter. This lets the narwhal detect changes in its environment, such as drops in temperature. Narwhals are some of the deepest-diving sea creatures and can dive more than 5,900 feet!

NORTHERN ELEPHANT SEAL
Mirounga angustirostris

These large seals make one of the longest migrations of any mammal, traveling up to thirteen thousand miles in one trip. The males are recognizable for the large, inflatable noses that hang about eight inches below their lower lip. Male **NORTHERN ELEPHANT SEALS** use their nose to make loud sounds to establish dominance and threaten other males. These noses are why elephant seals were named after elephants. Female elephant seals have a smaller nose. While on land, these seals use a belly-flop motion to crawl on sandy beaches.

OCEAN SUNFISH

Mola mola

This huge and flat silvery fish has only a few predators, such as sea lions and killer whales. This is due to its massive size. The **OCEAN SUNFISH** gains hundreds of pounds a year and can reach weights of up to five thousand pounds! The sunfish is a slow mover, swimming at only about two miles per hour. Even so, it is known to dive deep to hunt for its favorite meal: jellyfish.

FUN FACT: Though they are nicknamed killer whales, orcas are actually very large dolphins! The ocean is full of many oddly named creatures. The whale shark is also not a whale, even though it has *whale* in its name.

ORCA

Orcinus orca

Growing up to thirty-three feet long and twenty-two thousand pounds, **ORCAS** are some of the ocean's biggest creatures. These aggressive predators are curious and often approach humans to investigate. They live in small groups called pods and are very intelligent and playful. Orcas are powerful hunters and have had their hunting style compared to that of a pack of wolves. This might be how they earned their nickname: killer whales. Their black-and-white coloring helps them blend in with their dark, watery surroundings, giving them the perfect cover to hide while searching for their prey.

OLIVE RIDLEY SEA TURTLE

Lepidochelys olivacea

The smallest and most abundant of all sea turtles, these creatures can weigh up to one hundred pounds. This turtle gets its name from the olive-green coloring of its skin and heart-shaped shell. It tends to be a solitary animal (which means it likes to be alone) but will join a group of other **OLIVE RIDLEY SEA TURTLES** when it comes time to lay their eggs. They do this on sandy beaches. Then, hundreds of baby sea turtles hatch in the sand.

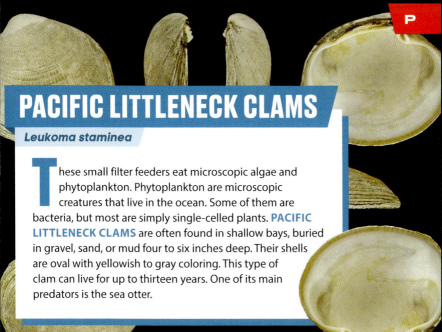

PACIFIC LITTLENECK CLAMS

Leukoma staminea

These small filter feeders eat microscopic algae and phytoplankton. Phytoplankton are microscopic creatures that live in the ocean. Some of them are bacteria, but most are simply single-celled plants. **PACIFIC LITTLENECK CLAMS** are often found in shallow bays, buried in gravel, sand, or mud four to six inches deep. Their shells are oval with yellowish to gray coloring. This type of clam can live for up to thirteen years. One of its main predators is the sea otter.

PACIFIC VIPERFISH

Chauliodus macouni

This silvery deep-sea fish uses its long, sharp teeth like a cage to trap prey. Two of its bottom front teeth are so long that they reach past the viperfish's eyes. The **PACIFIC VIPERFISH** has bioluminescent organs on its belly and moves to shallow waters at night to hunt. These fish reach one foot in length. The Pacific viperfish got its name because it is found in the waters of the North Pacific Ocean.

59

PARROTFISH

Scaridae

There are about eighty species of **PARROTFISH**, and they all come with special skills. Some species can change their color and even their gender. Other species of parrotfish have the ability to wrap themselves in a bubble of mucus to protect themselves from nocturnal predators. Some parrotfish have scales that are so strong they can stop a spear from piercing through. This type of brightly colored fish has a very important job: Parrotfish create coral reef sand. They use their beak-like teeth to bite off bits of coral to get to their favorite meal, algae. As they eat, they grind up and digest the bits of coral rock, too, pooping it back into the reef as sand.

PEARL OYSTER

Pinctada **spp.**

The **PEARL OYSTER** is most commonly found in warm coastal waters. They were cultivated as food for more than two thousand years and valued for the pearls that are often found in their shells. Despite popular belief, pearls don't typically form from a single grain of sand. Oysters are actually very good about pushing sand out of their shells. Pearls form when a small piece of foreign matter, like a parasite, enters the shell. The oyster then secretes the same materials that make up its inner shell, which surround the invader, protecting the oyster from it. Beautiful pearls are actually the product of an oyster practicing some incredible self-defense.

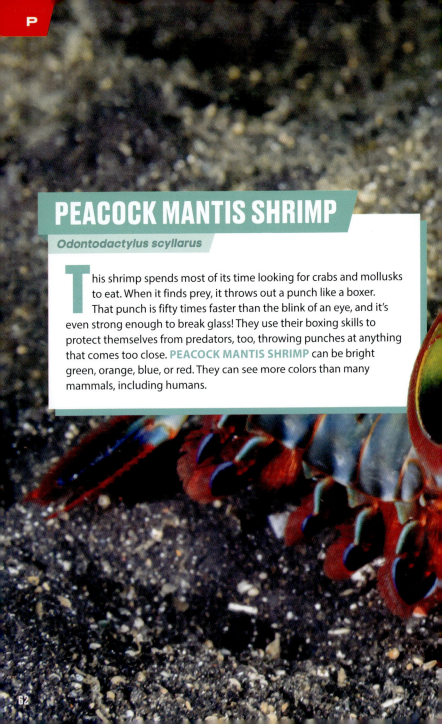

PEACOCK MANTIS SHRIMP

Odontodactylus scyllarus

This shrimp spends most of its time looking for crabs and mollusks to eat. When it finds prey, it throws out a punch like a boxer. That punch is fifty times faster than the blink of an eye, and it's even strong enough to break glass! They use their boxing skills to protect themselves from predators, too, throwing punches at anything that comes too close. **PEACOCK MANTIS SHRIMP** can be bright green, orange, blue, or red. They can see more colors than many mammals, including humans.

FUN FACT: The peacock mantis shrimp's eyes can see in two different directions at once!

PEPPERMINT SHRIMP

Lysmata wurdemanni

The **PEPPERMINT SHRIMP** is found off the coasts of Florida and in the Bahamas and the Caribbean. This small shrimp is named for the red and white markings on its body, making it look like a peppermint candy. Over its lifetime, this shrimp can change its coloring depending on what color light it is exposed to. Peppermint shrimp are known as cleaners because they feed on waste that other animals leave behind.

PINEAPPLEFISH

Cleidopus gloriamaris

With large yellow scales outlined in black, this fish got its name because it looks like a pineapple. These scales act as armor, but they also have consequences. **PINEAPPLEFISH** are not strong swimmers because of their small fins and the weight of their scales. These fish are native to Australia and can be found in reefs and harbors. Their lower jaws have bioluminescent organs that glow green, but the color of the light slowly becomes red as they age.

P

PINK SALMON

Oncorhynchus gorbuscha

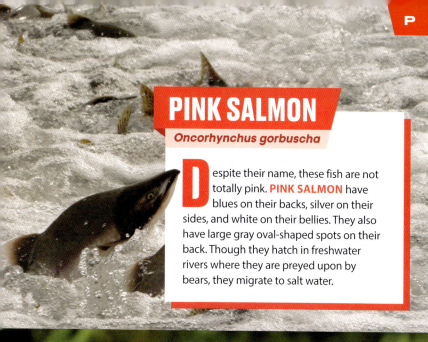

Despite their name, these fish are not totally pink. **PINK SALMON** have blues on their backs, silver on their sides, and white on their bellies. They also have large gray oval-shaped spots on their back. Though they hatch in freshwater rivers where they are preyed upon by bears, they migrate to salt water.

PINK SHRIMP

Farfantepenaeus duorarum

The **PINK SHRIMP** has ten walking legs and ten swimming legs. These shrimp bury themselves during the day and travel during the night, migrating to saltier water as they grow. They live in the Atlantic Ocean and are often found along the shores of the United States and Mexico. They can be found between the shores of Maryland and Texas. They can reach over eight inches in length, and females are typically larger than males.

PORTUGUESE MAN-OF-WAR

Physalia physalis

While it may look like one, this highly venomous predator is actually not a jellyfish at all. The **PORTUGUESE MAN-OF-WAR** is a colony made up of small individual zooids (which are clones) that cannot survive on their own and work together as one. The colony consists of a float to keep them at the sea's surface, tentacles for hunting small fish and crabs, and separate polyps for digestion and reproduction. The tentacles can be up to 160 feet long and deliver a powerful sting. These colonies like to float in groups, sometimes of a thousand or more. They can deflate their float and submerge underwater in case of danger on the surface. Instead of swimming, they use the wind and ocean currents to get around.

FUN FACT: The Portuguese man-of-war was named for its resemblance to eighteenth-century Portuguese warships.

PUFFERFISH

Tetraodontidae

These clumsy swimmers can inflate to become several times their normal size to escape predators. They fill their elastic stomachs up with water and air in order to blow themselves up. The toxic spines on the skin of some species of **PUFFERFISH** also help scare away predators. Their coloring depends on their diet and habitat, ranging from bright colors to muted whites and grays.

QUEEN ANGELFISH

Holacanthus ciliaris

This bright blue-and-yellow fish got its name from the blue crown on top of its head. Its bright coloring protects it from predators preying on the small, three-and-a-half-pound fish. The **QUEEN ANGELFISH'S** coloring also hides it from predators, helping it blend in with the colorful coral reefs where it lives.

RED LIONFISH

Pterois volitans

Most commonly found in coral reefs, the **RED LIONFISH** is a slow mover, sitting perfectly still while waiting to ambush its prey. It has up to eighteen red-and-white-striped dorsal fins that are venomous and used as protection against predators. While it doesn't use its venom against its prey, it does trap food by extending its jaw forward while it ambushes, allowing it to swallow its food whole.

REGAL BLUE TANG
Paracanthurus hepatus

Despite its name, the **REGAL BLUE TANG** starts out yellow as a baby and grows up to be blue with black markings and a yellow dorsal fin. These fish form schools for protection and use their venomous, sharp spines to ward off predators. They're found in coral reefs in the Indo-Pacific area, which includes the Philippines, Indonesia, Japan, Australia, and East Africa. Regal blue tangs also hunt in schools for algae. Their diet helps keep the algae growth on coral reefs under control, making them an important part of the ecosystem. Dory from Pixar's *Finding Nemo* is a regal blue tang.

SALTWATER CROCODILE

Crocodylus porosus

As the largest reptile on the planet, the **SALTWATER CROCODILE** reaches up to twenty-three feet in length and weighs over 2,200 pounds. It will eat just about any animal and has incredibly powerful jaws, with the strongest bite in the animal kingdom. It likes to lurk at the water's edge and pounce on its prey, dragging it into the water to drown it. Saltwater crocodiles have been around since the time of the dinosaurs.

SEA ANGEL *Clione limacina*

This creature is small in size and a graceful swimmer. It has no shell and can propel itself through the water by flapping its wings. The **SEA ANGEL** is actually a type of sea slug, though it is often mistaken for a jellyfish. This is probably because sea angels are mostly transparent, making them look similar to some types of jellyfish. They eat sea snails, and when they find one, they use the fingerlike tentacles on their heads to grab the prey, then use hook-like appendages to yank the prey from their shells.

SEA BUNNY

Jorunna parva

This sea slug might resemble a fuzzy bunny, but it isn't harmless. **SEA BUNNIES** are highly poisonous due to their preferred diet of toxic sea sponges, and they use the toxins they ingest to defend themselves against predators. Reaching up to one inch long, they have organs that look like little bunny ears on their heads, but the organs are not for listening. They are actually used to help these slugs find food and mates.

SEAHORSE

Hippocampus **spp.**

This creature got its name because its tiny head is the same shape as a horse's head. There are around fifty species of **SEAHORSES**. They use their small dorsal fin to slowly propel themselves forward and adjust the volume of air in their swim bladder, an air pocket in their body, to move up and down. They have a tail that they use to grab on to things and anchor themselves in place. Female seahorses lay up to a thousand eggs at a time, but male seahorses are the ones to carry their young in kangaroo-like pouches while they wait for them to hatch. Many people wrongly think that male seahorses give birth, but really the female seahorse's eggs are just hatching while being stored in the male seahorse's pouch.

FUN FACT: Sea otters entangle themselves in kelp forests to keep from floating out to sea. Sometimes, they even hold paws to stay together!

SEA OTTER

Enhydra lutris

SEA OTTERS are often found floating at the water's surface in forests of kelp or seaweed. While floating on their backs, sea otters can nap or use rocks to open up clams, mussels, and other shellfish to eat. They dive down to the seafloor to collect a rock that they use to break open the shellfish on their chests. After their meals, they take a bath, needing to keep their thick fur clean so that they can stay waterproof.

SEA STAR

Asteroidea

Like sea urchins and sand dollars, **SEA STARS** don't have backbones. The eyespots on the tips of their many arms help them find food. They can have anywhere from five eyespots to fifty! Their arms are covered in tiny suckers that help them slowly move along the seafloor. Parts of their bodies can actually regrow if lost in an attack, a process called regeneration. This means that if a sea star loses an arm, a new one will simply grow back in its place.

SEA URCHIN

Echinoidea

Nicknamed the porcupines of the sea, **SEA URCHINS** are covered in sharp spikes. They don't swim. Instead, they move along the seafloor, using tiny tube feet to slowly scoot around. Their mouth is on their underside, so while they move along, they eat up algae. Sea urchins are typically round and brightly colored, and some are even venomous.

SPERM WHALE

Physeter macrocephalus

The **SPERM WHALE** has the largest brain of any animal on earth! It can dive incredibly deep in search of squid to eat and can stay underwater for up to two hours at a time. Whales need to come up to the surface for air because they are mammals, so they need to breathe in oxygen. These creatures grow up to fifty-nine feet and can weigh up to ninety thousand pounds. Their most recognizable feature is their big, block-shaped head. Sperm whales were a huge target of the whaling industry in the United States because of a waxy substance, called spermaceti, found in their head. It was used in oil lamps and candles. While the hunting of sperm whales has decreased greatly, they still face threats today. They often die when they are struck by ships or caught in fishing nets. Because of this, sperm whales have been on the list of endangered species since 1970.

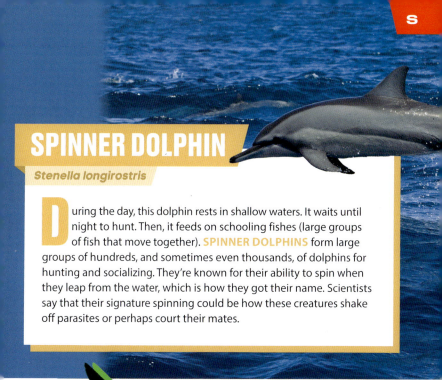

SPINNER DOLPHIN

Stenella longirostris

During the day, this dolphin rests in shallow waters. It waits until night to hunt. Then, it feeds on schooling fishes (large groups of fish that move together). **SPINNER DOLPHINS** form large groups of hundreds, and sometimes even thousands, of dolphins for hunting and socializing. They're known for their ability to spin when they leap from the water, which is how they got their name. Scientists say that their signature spinning could be how these creatures shake off parasites or perhaps court their mates.

SPINY DOGFISH

Squalus acanthias

When fishermen first observed the **SPINY DOGFISH** shark in their natural habitat, they compared the way the sea creatures moved to how packs of wild dogs move when they chase down prey. This doglike behavior earned them their name. Spiny dogfish sharks, which grow to be about four feet long, form large schools of hundreds and sometimes thousands of sharks. While spiny dogfish sharks are small in size, they are also mighty, using the venomous spines on their dorsal fins to protect themselves from bigger predators.

SPOTTED EAGLE RAY

Aetobatus narinari

The **SPOTTED EAGLE RAY** is most commonly found in shallow shore water such as bays and coral reefs. Named for its spotted markings, this ray can grow to be seven feet wide. It is a strong swimmer and can leap out of the water to fly through the air! It has a venomous spine on its tail that is uses in self-defense against predators.

STRIPED PYJAMA SQUID

Sepioloidea lineolata

The **STRIPED PYJAMA SQUID** is technically a species of cuttlefish and not a squid. Cuttlefish are different from squid because they have an internal shell called a cuttlebone. This special shell helps them stay buoyant as they travel through the sea. Striped pyjama squid live in the sand and mud of shallow coastal waters, burying themselves so only the top of their head and yellow eyes are visible.

SWORDFISH

Xiphias gladius

The **SWORDFISH** has a long bill that is flat and blunt, which it uses as a sword to slash at its prey. This is similar to how the Atlantic blue marlin hunts. The swordfish has a feature called a countercurrent heat exchanger, which is a special muscle used to warm its brain and eyes. This helps them hunt in deep, cold waters by allowing them to think fast and see more clearly. These fish can grow to be nearly fifteen feet in length and weigh one thousand pounds.

TIGER SHARK

Galeocerdo cuvier

The **TIGER SHARK** gets its name from the tigerlike stripe pattern on its sides. These stripes are extremely visible in young sharks but fade as they get older. As the fourth-largest shark in the world, the tiger shark can reach over twenty feet in length and weigh more than 1,400 pounds. They're known for eating everything and anything, including seabirds, turtles, stingrays, and even garbage. Some tiger sharks have even been found with tires and license plates in their stomachs.

VAMPIRE SQUID

Vampyroteuthis infernalis

The **VAMPIRE SQUID** is actually not a squid at all. It's a completely unique creature in its own category. It has eight arms, making it similar to a squid or octopus, but it doesn't have two tentacles like squid do. What it does have are two long armlike filaments that neither octopuses nor squid have. A filament is a long, skinny appendage on an animal that looks like a lengthy piece of thread. When vampire squid are threatened, they turn their webbed arms upside down, making it look like they're wearing a cloak. At the tip of each arm is a small amount of blue bioluminescence, making the creatures visible in the dark waters they call home.

VELVET BELLY LANTERNSHARK

Etmopterus spinax

This shark earned its name thanks to its bioluminescent black underbelly. The **VELVET BELLY LANTERNSHARK** is smaller than many other shark species. It grows to be only about eighteen inches long. It lives in deep ocean environments like the northeast Atlantic Ocean. Often, these small sharks are accidentally caught and killed by commercial fisheries (big businesses that catch fish to sell them). Because of this, some people are worried about the number of velvet belly lanternsharks left.

WALRUS

Odobenus rosmarus

These large foraging predators have three-foot-long tusks that are actually long canine teeth. Canine teeth are the four pointy, sharper teeth mammals have that help them bite. Humans have canine teeth! **WALRUSES** use these tusks to pull themselves out of the water and to create breathing holes in ice. In dangerous situations, walruses also use their tusks to protect their territory. Walruses have wrinkled gray skin covered in short red hairs. Their blubbery bodies can weigh up to 3,700 pounds. Blubber is the fat that sea animals have. Walruses can slow their heartbeats down to withstand the harsh, cold temperatures of the Arctic waters.

WEST INDIAN MANATEE

Trichechus manatus

Though these **MANATEES** are large, at around ten feet long and up to 1,200 pounds, they are also quite graceful. They like to spend time in shallow waters. As herbivores, they eat around 10 percent of their body weight in seagrass every day, which is about 120 pounds of grass daily. Their big appetites help seagrass beds stay healthy by keeping the grass short and maintained. Manatees spend ten to twelve hours a day sleeping and only swim at a speed of three to five miles per hour.

WHALE SHARK
Rhincodon typus

The **WHALE SHARK** is the largest fish in the world. It can grow to the size of a school bus. On average, whale sharks are between eighteen and thirty-two feet long. They are known for their broad, flattened heads and the checkerboard pattern along their sides and back, which is unique for each shark, like a human fingerprint. No two whale sharks have the same pattern. Despite their huge size, these fish are filter feeders and like to eat plankton, small schooling fish, and crustaceans. Their mouths are nearly five feet wide, and they suck in mouthfuls of water, straining out food. They are friendly and often interact with divers.

YELLOWFIN TUNA

Thunnus albacares

This torpedo-shaped fish is one of the fastest swimmers in the ocean, reaching speeds of nearly thirty miles per hour. It constantly swims with its mouth open in order to breathe and can swim across an entire ocean in a school of other tuna. YELLOWFIN TUNA can be extremely loyal to one another and will protect other yellowfin tuna when they are in danger.

YELLOW-LIPPED SEA KRAIT

Laticauda colubrina

These venomous snakes are named for the distinct yellow coloring on their faces. They spend most of their lives on land, digesting, resting, and nesting. They rub against rocks to help shed their skin. **YELLOW-LIPPED SEA KRAIT** snakes have a tail that they use like a paddle to help them swim when they are in the water hunting for eels to eat. They live in the warm waters of the western Pacific Ocean. These include the shores of countries such as Japan, China, the Philippines, and Indonesia.

YELLOW TANG

Zebrasoma flavescens

Found near the Hawaiian Islands, this bright yellow fish is an algae feeder and helps keep algae growth under control on coral reefs. They even help out sea turtles by eating the algae growth on their shells. One of the greatest threats to **YELLOW TANGS** is the destruction of their habitat by humans. Many different kinds of human-made destruction affect these tangs, including pollution, coral harvesting, snorkeling, and harmful fishing practices.

ZEBRA SHARK

Stegostoma tigrinum

Unlike some other sharks, the **ZEBRA SHARK** doesn't have to swim to breathe. During the day, it will rest on the ocean floor and face the current so the water pumps over its gills to help it breathe. It is nocturnal, so it can hunt at night, using the whisker-like organs on its snout to help it find prey deep inside coral reefs. Its long, flexible body wiggles like an eel to help it get into tight spaces while it hunts for its preferred snacks: crustaceans and mollusks.

RESOURCES

Built on the long legacy of TIME, TIME for Kids has been a trusted news source in schools for 30 years, providing educators with valuable resources for the classroom. From articles about new scientific breakthroughs to profiles on inspiring kids who are helping their communities, TIME for Kids has content to inspire every reader.

Learn more about sea creatures and other interesting animals with TIME for Kids!

Visit **www.timeforkids.com** and explore the **Animals** topic to discover your next favorite species.

FOR MORE INFORMATION ON SEA CREATURES, YOU CAN EXPLORE THE FOLLOWING WEBSITES:

MarineBio: www.marinebio.org/kids

National Ocean Service: oceanservice.noaa.gov/kids

National Wildlife Federation: www.nwf.org

Oceana: oceana.org/marine-life

SEE Turtles: www.seeturtles.org/kids

Shark Research Institute: www.sharks.org/kids-helping-sharks

World Wildlife Fund: www.worldwildlife.org